Tock-Tick-Tock,
The Mouse and the Clock

By Heather Reilly

© 2013 by Heather Reilly
All rights reserved. The book's author retains sole copyright to all intellectual contributions to this book, including but not limited to text and images.

No part of this publication may be reproduced, stored in a retrieval system, or transmitted in any form or by any means, electronic, mechanical, photocopying, recording, or otherwise, without written permission from the author.

ISBN: **978-0-9919367-4-8**

For Connor and Lily,
my two sparkling stars.

Tock-tick-tock,
all through the night,
goes the grandfather clock
in the pale moonlight.

Tock-tick-tock,
and then one **BONG!**
The grandfather clock
chimes its hourly song.

Tock-tick-tock,
in the quiet house,
the chimes at two
wake a tiny mouse.

Tock-tick-tock,
and *BONG!* three times,
the mouse looks out
as the big clock chimes.

Tock-tick-tock,
and out she creeps,
while the clock chimes four
and the house still sleeps.

Tock-tick-tock,
she finds some cheese,
then the clock strikes five,
and then…a…sneeze!

BONG! BONG! BONG! BONG! BONG!

AH
AH
AH-CHOO

*Tock-tick-tock,
look behind the chair,
the clock reads six,
but she's not there!*

Tock-tick-tock,
it's seven o'clock.
Now the kids are up,
the T.V. starts to squawk.

Tock-tick-tock,
and now it's eight.
The mouse gets a treat
that fell off a plate.

BONG! BONG! BONG! BONG! BONG! BONG! BONG! BONG! BONG!

Tock-tick-tock,
there are nine bongs now.
The cat tries to pounce
with a fierce "**Meow!**"

Tock-tick-tock,
The clock chimes ten.
It's time to go
back home again.

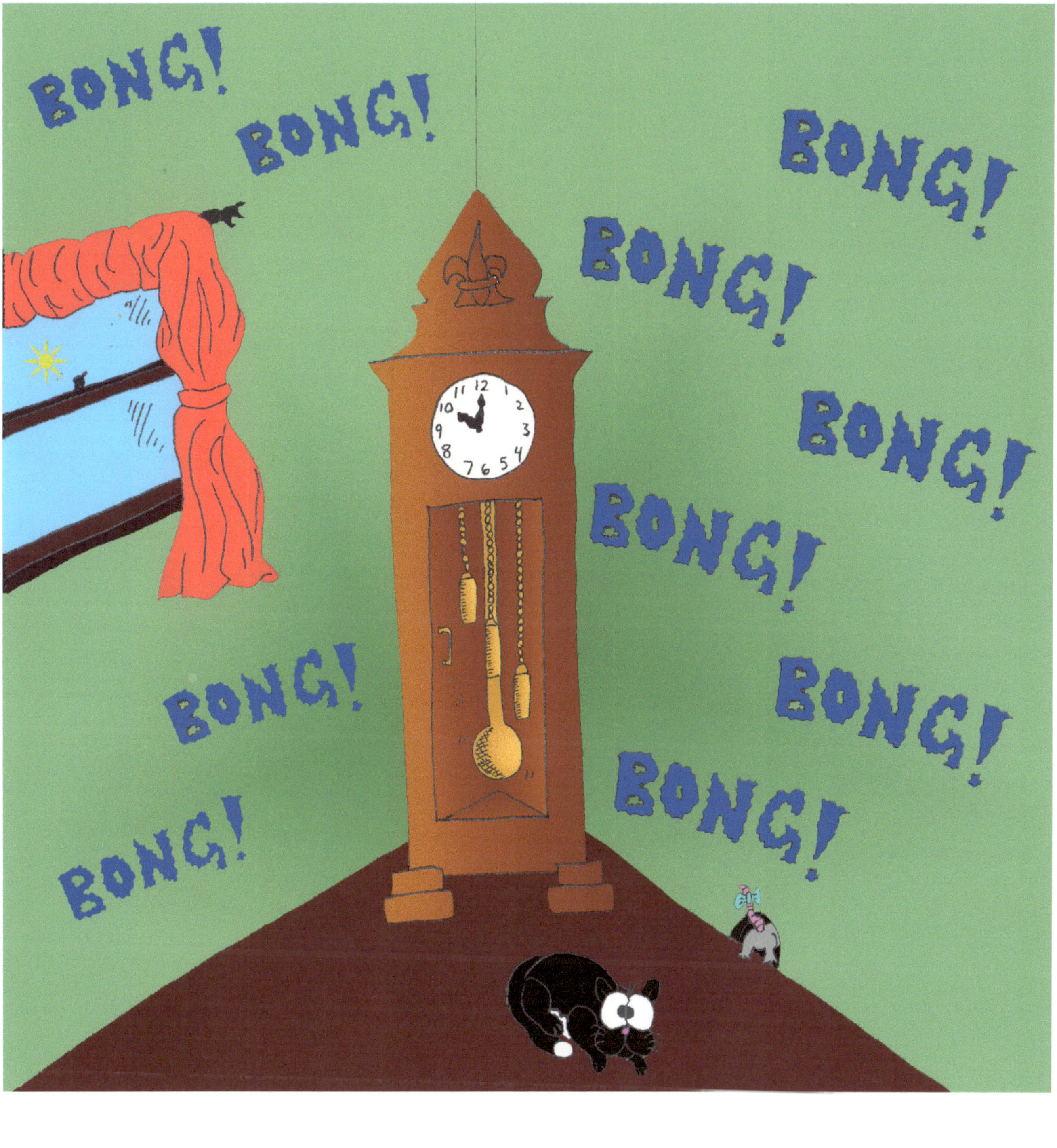
BONG!
BONG!
BONG!
BONG!
BONG!
BONG!
BONG!
BONG!
BONG!
BONG!

*Tock-tick-tock,
now she'll rest her head.
The time is eleven,
and she's back at her bed.*

BONG!
BONG!
BONG!
BONG!
BONG!
BONG!
BONG!
BONG!
BONG!
BONG!
BONG!
CRAYONS

*Tock-tick-tock,
and not a peep,
as the clock chimes twelve,
she's fast asleep.*

BONG! BONG! BONG! BONG! BONG! BONG! BONG! BONG! BONG! BONG! BONG! BONG!

Other books by Heather Reilly:

Novels:

Binding of the Almatraek
Book I: *Knight's Surrender*

Binding of the Almatraek
Book II: *Noble Pursuit*

Children's:

The Tree and the Sun

Upcoming Novels:

Binding of the Almatraek
Book III: *Enchanted Page*

Learn more about the author and her books at:
www.reillybooks.com

Titles are also available at amazon.com,
and on ebook at smashwords.com